T0354407

Speak Only Kindnesses

Speak Only Kindnesses

Volume 2: Directing the New Energy

TONI PAGE

BALBOA.
PRESS

A DIVISION OF HAY HOUSE

Balboa Press books may be ordered through booksellers or by contacting:

Balboa Press
A Division of Hay House
1663 Liberty Drive
Bloomington, IN 47403
www.balboapress.com
1 (877) 407-4847

Print information available on the last page.

ISBN: 978-1-5043-9330-0 (sc)
ISBN: 978-1-5043-9331-7 (hc)
ISBN: 978-1-5043-9329-4 (e)

Library of Congress Control Number: 2017918175

Balboa Press rev. date: 01/30/2018

PREFACE

Speak Only Kindnesses

My story is a simple story. I was changed. Changed by a set of events that, despite my resistance, was to benefit me beyond belief. I do not pretend to understand the mechanics, the who, how or why. I hope this book also changes you.

I was raised Catholic. I gave it up for Lent one year, in 6th grade. I never returned to the organized religion but continued to seek a spiritual connection through an insatiable predilection for reading material that was on the fringe of both spirituality and metaphysics.

My story is about the heart. I had experienced so much heartbreak over such a long period of time, that my heart closed. Yes, I went through the motions: I loved briefly and intensely, and repeatedly, but the unconditional love that originates in the heart was not to be found.

My father died of a heart valve that closed. I was 9. With my first pregnancy, I learned that I, too, inherited a congenitally defective aortic valve….and my valve was closing and would need to be replaced. I managed to delay the open heart surgery until I was 55 by judicious diet, exercise and heart-healthy supplements. I underwent the gruesome surgery in 2010. I became conscious midway through the operation but could not speak or move. Traumatized, I gave up and succumbed to the last sleep. Unexpectedly, however, I woke in pain, groggy, disgruntled and ornery. I had lost my right lung function, had a poorly functioning heart, and could neither walk nor talk normally for months. My esophagus randomly went into noisy spasm. The broken wired-together breastbone hurt relentlessly, and I could not sit up for months without muscle spasms in my back and neck delivering excruciating pain. I remember, as clearly as I remember yesterday, waking alone in the middle of each night, sweating, in pain, and disoriented, with a disgusting medicinal taste in my mouth. It was nearly 9 months before I was able to breathe, walk, talk and return to my work. I vowed I would never undergo such a surgery again. When this valve exhausted its lifetime, I exhausted mine. It was certain.

I did not have an easy time during the years following my surgery. In fact, I was not "nice", I became depressed, fell into bankruptcy, lost resources I had saved over a lifetime, lost my partner to an early death, and came close to losing my job, a career for which I had spent eons in training. I began sleeping 15 -18 hours most days and this went on for about 7 months, jeopardizing my health, social connections and career. I did little else.

Then, the news. The aortic heart valve implanted 5 years before was a bad model. It was failing. I had two months to live. Or, I could agree to the unthinkable – having another surgery, a "re-do". Anesthesia, analgesics, tearing out the old wires and rebreaking the sternum, cutting out the old scar tissue and extricating the bad valve. Stitching in a new one. Pain, disorientation, bedrest, dozens of medications and blood draws, loss of appetite. High risk, uncertain outcome, possibility of permanent life changes.

There was little time for deliberation. I sought guidance from friends, relatives, neighbors, physicians, my sons. I sought guidance from psychic readers, spiritual advisors, the pendulum, kinesiology. I prayed to God, spiritual Guides, and Angels. I turned within. I prepared to go into surgery not caring whether I lived or died. It didn't really matter that much.

And then I had the visions. I can't say when they began. They were with me before during, and after surgery. The image was clear and familiar from my childhood. It was Christ in front of me, slightly to my right, in his soft white robes with his gentle eyes and long brown hair. He was holding out in front of him a new heart ...one that was radiating a brilliant white light, and a warmth that was connecting us. I would continue life in this body, provided I chose to share His teachings. I would be gifted with a new heart, and the energy of youth, if I agreed to speak only kindnesses from that day forward. Was this an agreement, a commitment, a contract? I had a new purpose. His message is to bring others to awareness that there is Divinity within each of us, and we are more powerful than we realize.

I woke from surgery in only mild discomfort and was ecstatic!!! I was joking and laughing with my sister and son as soon as the breathing tube was removed! I joyfully told the cardiac surgeon how great I felt! I was breathing fine within hours. My pulse and blood pressure stabilized. My heart rhythm was entrained by cardioversion. I was surrounded by people that I loved and who loved me. I felt my Spiritual team around me every minute of the days that followed. The love energy was palpable. A dear friend saw legions of Angels surrounding me. I experienced a miraculous recovery as I continued to have the vision of Christ offering me the glowing heart each night after surgery, even after I returned home. Within days, I was walking, eating, unmedicated, happy, alert, talking with my loving friends and family of caregivers. I was very conscious and appreciative of my new open, radiating heart. I felt love for whomever fell into my view. I was moved to tears by compassionate actions of those around me, of people in the news. I wept while watching movies. I felt my heart open to friends and strangers alike. I felt more in the days after surgery than in the decades before.

At seven weeks I drove myself to Chicago. At 8 weeks post-surgery I was doing what it took 8 months to manage after the first aortic valve replacement. I felt energetic, strong, healthy and ecstatic to be in my physical body. I have learned how to re-image myself and rejuvenate. Each day I am more connected to and appreciative of all those around me, both physical and non-physical Beings.

I am not the same person I was. I am more loving. I am at peace. I am kinder, patient and accepting. I am more joyful, confident and secure. I have a knowing of my purpose. I gratefully relinquish my previous scientific career for one that involves teaching, comforting and healing others. I have changed and I believe that change is attributable to my encounters with the Christ, the Master, the Teacher. My new heart represents the Christ within. And the Christ is within each of us. We need only remember to ask that he speak with us.

I believe that the words in this book are His.

T. Page

PROLOGUE

As I sit quietly, first thing in the morning, I receive one-word-at-a-time messages that I write down in my journal. I 'hear' these messages whenever I invite Christ to tell me what I need to know; to teach me what he would have me teach. I have been writing now, most mornings, for over a year. When I read the messages I am struck by how new the words feel, like I have never heard them before. I am also amazed that the messages are coherent, loving, and, for me, inspiring. In the spirit of weaving together a kinder, more tolerant world, I share these messages with you.

Collectively, these volumes shall be known as "New Teachings of Christ the Life Source".

Surrounded by Light

1

Encompass Others in Your Love

Poetry is the song of life to the Poet. Love is the source of life to the devout. What is meant by 'devout,' here, is not what is typically understood. Here, it is used as a description of all those who recognize and honor the self, love the self and seek to encompass others in that love. As the love is shared, there births a larger, more grand entity, both in the physical and in the spiritual domain. So, do not hesitate to show, to feel, to share or to send your love. For in doing this you are able to create and gift the world. Be confident that only good comes of this. Be confident that in the sharing of love you, too, are encompassed in a beautiful stream of the Life Source.

2

Know the Kindness of Your Creator

Life is kind. The Source of All Creative energy has no wants or needs. Thus, there is nothing to predispose human life to be anything other than what humans choose to experience. Many religions have put forward the idea that God, in all the conceptualized forms, has a desire to bring pain and suffering. There is no point to this belief, for all that humanity experiences flows into the eternal awareness of Creator. For all that is said and done, by and to each of you, is transmitted to the awareness of "God". Why would that God have any desire to hurt his Creations; to harm, torment or torture with daily small deaths of disillusion and disappointments?

Understand, Dear Ones, it is not your God that chooses your unhappiness, but you...in each thought, pain, acknowledgement of evil...each act of choice defines you in this existence. Be the one who knows of the kindness of your Creator. Be the one who can fully trust in the benevolence of your God. While God would have it no other way, you, My Children, have placed your fury, your base expectations on Creative Source. Know, too, that you can change your experience of life. It is simple, so simple in fact many of you, particularly Christians, dismiss it entirely. Know now that it is merely pure trust and belief that your world is kind, your Creator, benevolent and your choice unerring. Go, be at peace. Trust that there is only beauty in Creation and make it that way.

3

Humanity's Claims are Hollow

All spiritual practices are valid and enrich the hearts of those who embrace the practices fully. Many of you children, in the arms of your mother, were first blessed with the Light of God on your forehead - the third eye, your crown chakra and your heart. At that time, the connections were made to allow Spirit to talk to you and through you. As you aged, it is true that many of you became more rewarded for cerebral efforts than matters of the heart. And, so that was for a purpose. As you have given of yourself through your pursuits as man has taught you, you have become aware of the hollowness of humanity's claims. It has been a journey for you to accept the veracity and the credibility of the magnificence of a heart-centered life. You have, and will continue to witness and experience the contrast between the rigid messages of science and the warm, understanding and flexible messages of the heart. You will know instinctively how to live, communicate your and My messages, and to reach out from the heart. There are so many, even in your life, who have never taken the outstretched hand of God, of Christ, of kind Spirit. They know not the comfort and hope of living in the now, knowing they are taken care of for all eternity. There shall be clearly manifest hope for those who are open, those who call

4

upon the Christ, those who are open and believing that there is a kinder and better path to follow. As this new energy blesses all, it is those who ride upon the waves of change readily and with full trust in a benevolent God that will realize joy first. May you and all those you touch be among the faithful to touch the face of God.

Waves of Change

4

Change Now

On the surface, your lives appear to be filled with duress. You move from one task to another without thinking about whether those tasks serve you in any way. Yet, when you are presented with opportunities to change your life, your perspective, your goals - you inevitably reach for what you had. Recognize, Children, that when adversity falls upon you, that it is an invitation to change. Stop before you react. Feel the message the adversity brings to you. Consider what the feelings are that will transport you to a place of calm, of security, of love. Dwell on those feelings. And, if you listen to your heart during those times of quiescence you will hear the answer. I warn you now, that in many instances that answer will be "change now". For the manner in which you reach to me will assist you in attaining your highest good. You are loved beyond measure. Share it.

5

See Rainbows of Light

On the edge of a rainbow there is a zone of refractive brilliance. This is the crystallized water that forms the strip in the sky that breaks apart light into different wavelengths, or colors, so that you see the beauty of what colors lie within white or clear light. As this occurs, the light itself does not change. It is merely by looking at the light from a different view you are able to see the rainbow. This is the way spiritual growth is, as well. For as one becomes more facile in looking at the light all around you, in all its forms, the better you become at seeing things from different angles. Spiritual growth is when you learn to view from the angle at which you see only the rainbows, only the bright true colors that comprise the light. In everyone you meet see the rainbows. Keep searching, look from different perspectives, look with new glasses on but look knowing that everything and everyone in the physical is comprised of a rainbow of light. Once you are able to see the beauty and harmony of your world, even more colors will be added to your rainbows. Be prepared to be surprised. Be joyful, for as you begin to see the lovely colors and point them out for others, you bring more light, more peace and more harmony into the world. Be at peace knowing you are greatly loved beyond measure. Share your love, your light, your peace. Do it by yourself. Do it when you are with others. Do it consciously. Know your power. It is all that comes through you.

Patterns of Rainbow Light

6

Male and Female are Blending

There is a shift. A shift in the light that mankind holds in this Universe. And, for the next decade, that shift will become apparent in the lives of men and then apparent to the women. For women are born with a tighter tether to Spirit. This is what allows the entry of new life into the wombs of many. For those who are open to connecting with their Divinity are those who understand the beauty and value of life....all life. Men, however grand and sensitive, have a less firm tether to their Higher Self. They are more grounded in Earth's base and this allows their greater willingness to protect and manage the resources for their young. It is an extension of the instincts of the animals on your planet. Both aspects of humanity are essential and grand and neither can stand alone. In this new energy, the aspects of man that have held his hand to the fire, have thrust the battle swords upon him will melt away. For those aspects no longer serve either him or the women and children of his life. It will be evident to many who are older and have lived longer in the old energy. It will come naturally to those children born into the new energy. And you will see more and more of the blended being born - blended male and female physically, cognitively, in mind and in Spirit. Welcome these new children with open arms, for they are manifestations of your will to live in peace, blended across cultures, races, and now, sexes and genders. It is a homogenization of the physical. However, be aware that each entity, each life is totally unique and on the path of its own choosing. Respect those new paths and welcome the new mankind - a mix with womankind. Remember the love is to be shared.

7

Light and Love Sustain Life

I am the energy of the Light. As such, I power life with the substance of love. And all living things are powered, brought into being, and sustained by light and love. Humans are no exception. To be full and whole, each of My Children thrives best when there is a quiet cycle of Light and dark. Each of My Children is nourished by this quiet cycle of Light and dark, for it is what allows the growth of crops, the feed for your animals and the recycled life that enriches the soil of Gaia. As it is with Earth, so is it with humankind. A cycle of Light and dark works best to allow growth. It is at this time you will flow into a brief but dark phase of your cycle of growth My Dear Ones. Trust that it, too, is short and will move into Light again. That you can count on, as you know morning starts anew each day. And with each day there is more new growth; bit by bit, slowly but surely, a mature crop will emerge.

What is it that sustains during the dark when there is the appearance of no Light? It is the love the Light leaves behind in its wake and the love that shines through your planet Earth even as you cannot see the Sun on the other side. During the coming period of dark, know you will emerge. And, do not dismay for there are great joyful days that are ahead. This is a time of growth. This is a time to feel and reflect the essence of the love that is pulsed to you with every heartbeat, every breath, every movement. I speak to you to give you comfort. I ask for your trust. I urge you to begin each day by feeling the unmeasurable love that flows to you and through you. Become accustomed to this feeling, this power, this connection to the Whole, for it is your power to move mountains. Use the love in your heart. Share the love in your heart. And, you will create a new world in the new energy that will surpass even your wildest dreams of peace and abundance. Harmony will be imposed on All. This is as your hearts sing as one in praise to the Divinity within All of You.

8

Sound Transforms

You are soothed by the sound of song. It is all around you, but you may not hear. It is in the air, it is reverberating in the oceans, it moves through your bodies, it keeps the Earth spinning in orbit. Sound is transformative. Song is euphorigenic. Vibrations of sound can shatter physical objects or put a heart into a new rhythm. Sound is enveloping. If it is used wisely, it will soothe your being. Or, it can uplift your spirits, or it can inspire you to new levels of thought and Being. The "Om...." is one good example of a calming and uplifting vibration. If you practice it routinely you will experience greater calm, more stability in your mind. When the mind is calm and clear, it becomes much easier to hear the voice of Spirit. However, the voice of Spirit is not delivered with the vibration of sound, for sound is in your physical world and consists of vibration of air. No, the sound of Spirit is also of vibration but a vibration in the realm of the non-physical. There is no air or medium through which to pass. Only the high vibratory ethers that connect you to the Higher Self can be the receiver of the voice of Spirit. Go there. Go there frequently in your meditations, in your prayers, as you sing or as you walk the paths on Mother Gaia. Go to that place in your vibration where you can "hear" the voice of

Spirit. Every human can. All that is needed is the intention to commune with the Greatest Good and your Higher Self. Be not shy, for you are invited to accompany Spirit every day, in all ways. Listen carefully and you will hear the peace and love that is yours.

9

Know You are Well

Sickness, in Truth, is a symptom. Do not accept blame or feel remorse if you are not well, or experience long-term illness or conditions. The circumstances are not of your making. Not directly. But, most certainly, indirectly. Listen now, that you may avert the circumstances that translate into all manner of sickness. The human is not at all confident of his or her ability to set intention to be well and see it manifest. This, which is your birthright, is undermined by the bombardment of your minds to a constant stream of messages. These messages are on TV, the radio, in your kitchens, and they tell you that you are not in control. This is false. As you believe, so it will come to pass. Believe in your perfect health. Pay attention to your well-being. If you require aids such as medicines to encourage this belief, then use those aids. Whatever assistance you require to adjust your belief is useful.

Sickness is not an uninvited condition. Rather it is a symbolic form of one's resignation to what appears inevitable. This is a misunderstanding. For all circumstances that present in your life can be changed. If you come to realize you feel trapped in a situation, you will develop sickness that is symbolic of restrictions on your movements. If you feel you are not worthy of that which life bestows or asks of you, your energy will be depleted and you will not be able to use or taste the sweetness of life. For all conditions, temporary or chronic, there is a belief at its basis. Look deeply into your beliefs and learn what the sickness offers. As there is little to be gained by anyone by being ill, recognize that rarely does sickness serve anyone. Know your beliefs. Know where your vulnerable beliefs are. Address them with open choices, alert attention to how you feel and depend on and trust your body to lead you out of sickness and out of whatever circumstances caused your "adaptation". Be patient, but trusting in yourself to lead you. For those who have suffered for a long time, it is more difficult to see and understand the causes. Know that you are in control. Tell your body, your cells how you want it to be. Trust your body hears you, and as your beliefs change, so will your illness. It is important to know and practice changing your beliefs. There is no desire on the part of God to burden any of His Children with illness except those who have chosen it. Know you are loved beyond measure. Ask me, the Christ, to lead you to a place of wellness. Love is healing and so the first step in this process is to feel genuine and moving love for yourself. Play with this awhile. Feel it. Announce it. Express it in all you do. Shortly you will see benefits.

Expressions of Divinity Within

DAY 10

Love Empowers Creation

All religions are the same. All humanity seeks to ritualize what they believe is the "right way" to love God. What is only now being realized is that there is a "unique" and "right way" for each entity incarnated in human form. Each soul reaches out in its own manner to connect with Creative Source. For one, the truest line of communication may be with art, another music, another prayer, and yet another, asceticism. Each religion of this planet was founded with inspiration from the Masters. But, each Master had his or her own unique form of expression of their Divinity BECAUSE each expression of Divinity IS unique. So, you see, My Children, look not upon your neighbor's religiosity or lack of religiosity with judgment or disdain. But, look at your neighbor's unique expression and realization of the spark of God that is temporarily housed within his or her body.

Even as you put names to large groups who claim to adhere to one worship system, such as Muslim, Buddhist, Hindu or Christian, the manner of worship, belief, behavior and expression that resides within the group is as varied as mankind, itself. There is no "one, true religion", for all forms of acknowledging God and your Divine connection to God are valid. There is no doctrine that was written by

God, only words delivered in each time period of Earth's maturation to comfort, guide, and allow humanity to ponder their relation in that time period. So it is now. For these words are delivered with the intention of focusing your beliefs and your knowledge into a different realm from your past. The new energy of the ascending Earth allows a more gracious encounter of humankind with their Spirits, their Higher Selves, which are expressions of Source Energy. On this night, Christmas Eve on the calendars and electronic calendars of many, let there be a greater understanding that all of My Children are of one parent, all expressions of the same consciousness to differing degrees, All as equally loved by the Creative Source as your own children. Let the perceived differences among religious identities fall away with the realization that all expressions of love are part of the essence of God. Let the peace and joy and comfort that all humanity strives for be found in the knowing that you are loved beyond measure. That love is unlimited, unending and unqualified. There is enough love to last all eternity. It can only grow, not diminish. I invite you of all religions to taste the love, share the love that is Mine, All of Ours, with each other and watch it grow. Watch it creep slowly across the Earth, one person at a time, one family at a time, one Soul group at a time. One kindness, one gentle word, one welcoming gesture, one thank you, at a time, will move all of My Children, with ease and grace, to the blessed family dinner table. For as Christmas approaches, I ask each of you to look into your hearts and feel, really feel, the love that empowered the creation of your world. Now it is your opportunity to use the love in your hearts to mold, to shape, and to enliven the world the way you want yourselves and your children to live in it.

See the sky tonight. For I and each man and woman are created anew in each dawn. Be in peace. Know the comfort of God Source's love, and, forget the pain. Rather, live in your beautiful bodies, indulge on occasion, and celebrate the "Wonders of His Love".

Wonders of His Love

11

Tap Into Your Power

The pictures you have seen of My Sacred Heart are an accurate depiction. My heart is ablaze with the White Light of God-Source. It ruled me, then when I was in man-form. It rules me now, as I am a streak of energy that crosses dimensions and can enter into your hearts. You, Dear Ones, can allow the energy from my heart to merge with yours. In doing so the power and the glory of God-Source becomes amplified through you. This is a state of 'Being', a transformative process, not something that occurs at once. But this transformation is available to All My Children upon their asking. It is with great love I have offered this option to Each of You. You will know when and if you are ready for me to join you from the spiritual into the physical in this manner. On this Christmas Day, I send you, My Children, the message that you, too, have been born sons and daughters of All-That-Is. There is little difference between who I became and who you may will yourself to Be. There is Mastery in each of you, there for the asking, for the calling, for the stepping into your true power. None of you are singular. Each of you is a mere tiny extension into the physical of an enormous majestic energy flow of the Universe. You have full rights to tap into your power. But there is a secret law of access. The power is kept hidden to all those who do not take the time to find the key. For those who know they want access are guided through Source to their feelings. It is the conscious and extensive and deep emergence of the vibration of love and compassion and appreciation that serves as the key to open the door to the majesty of your power as Creators. Do not take these words as frivolous. For in each word there is truth. In each conception there is that which should be learned, known and felt. As My Children choose, they will receive. As my children choose My Sacred Heart energy as their guide they become more facile in moving the energy of love around in this world. Soon, My Children, you will begin to realize the power your expressions of love have over the physical components of your World. Soon, you will learn to have great impact on transitioning this Earth into a truly magical and magnificent creation. Be steady. Be in My Graces. For you are loved beyond measure, and therefore the energy available to you for creation is unlimited. May the love of Christmas spur you on to your personal path of creation for the Highest Good.

12

Speak to Spirit With Your Thoughts

Speak to me and with me every day. Even though you cannot see, or typically hear me, I am there to hear your voice, your thoughts. Yes, thoughts are real, tangible, communicative. They are energy, just as the electromagnetics of your heart are energy. You think little about the medical practice of requiring an electrocardiogram to measure and record the health of your heart muscle. But, rarely do you ever think that the electromagnetics of your brain can be measured to tell you the health of that organ. Think on this. For as one experiences joy, fun, love and is of service to mankind, there is a strong, cyclic and rhythmic pulse to the brain, mirrored by positive, loving, hopeful and optimistic thoughts. When the acts are not of such great harmony, when one seeks comfort in drugs, eats for self-pleasure, becomes self-centered, then the rhythms and cycles of the brain become disordered, desynchronized. As this occurs, it lends to expressions of thoughts of depression, worthlessness, hatred, anger. And, as these thoughts emerge they feed back on the brain to produce more disruption. All of this, Child, is easier to "read" than you might think. I can feel, I can hear and know the energy of your thoughts. For this is the wave upon which my communications render. When you come to speak with me each day I can listen, I can provide comfort and can communicate without the necessity of words. When you speak with me, you are more readily aligned with the path of communication that is the same wavelength as mine. You can be more open, more vulnerable and receive the knowledge that you need, each day, to assist you to maintain an open heart, think thoughts of kindness and joy. As this is your practice, soon it will be with ease that you adopt the path of the Masters. For, in the knowing and in the direction of your thoughts, you are able to sustain a state of "Being" of your own choosing. This act of choosing your thoughts has formative power. Thoughts of fear form a personality structure that supports fearful behavior. Thoughts of courage form a mindset that enacts courageous behaviors. Thoughts of generosity enable the abundance that flows to sustain the characteristics of generosity. So, Child, speak to me of your thoughts each day. Speak with me of the best or Highest thoughts you can express. Together, we will travel on a course of comfort and joy, as you learn to be at peace with your thoughts and manifest that which you choose. This is the way of it. I will always be here for you. Speak freely. Speak to me, always, in your thoughts.

13

You Can Never Be "Without"

I am home. I am in the brilliance of God Source. Now, Always.
You, too, share a piece of my home in all its beauty. You resonate
here with the joyous song. You bring comfort to all and adore the
grandness of the Beings on earth, of which you are a part. Come
with me on this journey home, where you will feel and know the
ecstasy of a truly free life. Be not afraid of losing that which you
WILL lose. Be not afraid of opening the heart which you WILL
open. Be not afraid of giving away and sharing all that you have
to give, for you WILL pass it on, eventually. Come home with me.
Come in love and trust. Come join me near the warm fireside.
For in that peace of home, Child, you will discover and take to
your breast all that you have owned, loved, touched, released and
shared. It has all become part of you. You will retain it for all
eternity like a photo but better. You cannot lose your experiences
for they live in your Akash on and on. Know, then, Dear One,
that you can never be "without" as long as you realize the wealth
of the experience that travels with you across many lives that no
one can take away. Ever.

14

Honor Your Youth

Warring must stop. All forms of battle must come to a halt before my presence can be fully felt as the Prince of Peace. There will be peace on earth. As one method to achieve this, there will come a time when all cultures, all races demonstrate a true understanding of the power of love. The soldiers will be some of the first to fully appreciate the bliss of peace. For the soldiers around the world live in fear and unrest, even as they sleep. The contrast between their time of 'duty' and the small but successful steps they take to preserve the little peace they find will magnify their intentions to strive for peace. Love of family will be an important value and experience. All family - blood, adoptive, and chosen. The nurture of peace and love will whet the appetites of soldiers both by their own experience but also by bearing witness to the love and peace that much of the world already knows. They see that they ache for the comforts of home. They crave the touch of a warm and loving partner. They only must be given the opportunity to choose a peaceful way of life. Fewer and fewer men and women will volunteer for military duty in virtually all countries. The youth of this new energy period will not be born with the "vampire's" thirst for blood. For they will come forward with new knowledge of peace and a remembrance of their past lives to a greater extent. They will be born with the knowing that there is only futility in warring as there is no winner in any battle; no side comes out untouched. These youth of the new energy will understand that peaceful resolution and cooperation yields a much bigger and better "payout". So, as these youngsters become emboldened to express their new energy, do not hold them back. They have the power and the will to live in a more welcoming and easier world. They will bring the change that they envision. They will run over the current politics and laws to bring more effective practices into being. Recognize this is as it should be in the natural progression toward peace on this planet. Know, also, that it is with the love and support of all humans that the youth will be successful translators of love into peace for All. Go now, and honor your youth.

15

Learn to Feel

Settle-in. Use this day as an opportunity for deep prayerful meditation. Now that you have a taste of the comfort and feeling that comes with allowing the acceptance of your Divine connection, you need some period of time to settle into this new state of realization. I guide you to proceed through your day making every action a prayerful action. Those that do not "fit" or resonate with your prayerful countenance may not be fruitful or in the Highest Good. Learn to feel and recognize the difference. All actions taken in harmony with your Divinity within will "feel" good and right and will produce no discord in your consciousness. Actions taken that deviate from your path will not be as comfortable and will produce some measure of conscious reluctance or dismay. Know that this is the Divine guiding you closer to the Being YOU have chosen to BE. All aspects of your Divinity participate in these choices and you, My Dear One, are not always ready to see those choices. It is of little matter because, at some time, it will come into fruition. As you choose, so you are guided by many who assist you, on your path. You can choose to take detours my Dear, but you cannot fall off your path.

Rest quietly a time before you initiate the actions of your day. Sit with each action and feel whether it resonates with your Inner Being. Feel the difference and learn to apply this method, this tool, to the choices you make each day. It is a practice that will result in you moving at a much faster pace to where you want to Be.

Your Path

16

Fear Disempowers

My Loved Ones, let your heart guide you in all that you do. Place your awareness not behind your eyes, but deep in your chest. Feel the connections to all parts of your body. Feel your connections to the energy of the heart - the rhythm, the pulse, the pushing out of energy from the source. The heart is a miniature representation of the energy that is 'pushed out' from God-Source. Each pulse flows to and through all creation, much like your blood flows to all tissues, all cells. The energy of God-Source is transformed as it passes through the Universe, some into streams of consciousness, some into matter, some into humans and other Beings or animals. The heart's blood, too, is transformed into energy better suited to nourish cells with oxygen and clear fluids. And, as the energy is used for growth, sustenance and reproduction, the unusable bi-products are ejected, washed away or exhaled to become a cyclic part of the units of Creation. Now, in your world, you face the clearing away of the unusable bi-products of thousands of years of mankind's struggles against itself. There is no longer any benefit to killing one's enemy. There is no longer any benefit to stealing away food from another. The world has become a place where a small portion of humans can and are knitting together a community that will no longer tolerate such injustices. They will expose and move such persons out of the way and they will continue doing their good. Remember, as those of the darkness begin to clear themselves from Earth, that there is no reason to fear. Fear brings more fear, greater fear, and stops your power to love. Don't give into the fear or the grief that will steal your innate power from you. Know your will, your preferences, for they that choose wisely may live in peace, even among those who only see and experience chaos. In this new year, feel the energy as it pulses through you and guide it with love in your heart to create the world the way you want it to be. And do this with the full knowledge that Creative-Source will help you on your path. Be at peace. Be trusting. Be full of hope, for your future is brilliant.

17

Men and Women Balance the Planet

This Year is a time of trial. It is a year when blood will be shed. It is a year when humanity will begin to agree jointly on what they choose their world to look like...a war-devastated zone or a garden of peaceful bliss and loving cooperation. From this place of Being, the choices have become clear. And You, my Children, will usher in this new Era of peace. I am the Life Source and so it is through I, the Christ, that you may realize the path to this garden of joy, the garden Creative Source has always meant for you to enjoy. Ah, yes, this is reminiscent of the Creation story - one very appropriate in your year of the New Energy. Yes, Creative Source seeded your planet and only beauty and peace reigned. But because you have been gifted with free will your choices soon led you farther from your close connection with Source. You, some of you, began to choose to cut off the benevolent energy of your Life Source and to create dark energy flows that infiltrated the minds of man and to a lesser extent, women. This difference in the ability to accept dark energy between men and women comes from the tighter tether that women come onto the Earth with. They are more closely bound to Source Energy because they must be allowing of Life Source to penetrate them to bring new life, babies to your Earth. And so, that is not to say one sex is more light or one filled with more darkness, for each of you, Children, have been both in male and female bodies many times. There is a balance of energies that works out over thousands of years. And, that is why there are always fewer males on the planet at any one time, than females. It is to preserve Gaia and the overall energetic tone of Earth. As the tethers of your women become tighter - more closely aligned with Source Energy, you will see more and more men follow in the footsteps of the women in their lives.

You will see more men ready to demonstrate peaceful ways, compassion, kindness, service and unquestioning love. As the earth energy absorbs this shift, there will become more of a balance of males and females. This will show itself readily in professions like medicine and law, nursing and the clergy. These balancing effects will also help move all closer to the realization that peace and love and bounty are more to be desired than hatred, war and scarcity. Move forward in this new, gentle energy, and give only thoughts and feelings of love and compassion to those who have chosen to be less in this lifetime. Go knowing your year will be kind and, while there will be many painful trials, there is great movement toward a peaceful Earth. You are loved beyond measure. Share it and spread it across Earth as though you are the Sun, lighting up the planet fresh and new each dawn. So be it.

18

Amplify Your Well-being

Be kind to your body. Your body is the mastery of the expressions of life, as it has developed on Earth today. Bodies are conglomerates of cell types, tissue, organs and structures that are all tied together with a streamlined communication system. That system is electromagnetic expression of love. The fields of the DNA in your cells intersect and interact with the fields of adjacent cells until the whole body knows what the question is your biologists forgot to ask. How can DNA that is physically separate from other DNA direct the growth and maturation and maintenance of such a complex body? There is never such a thing as the "left hand not knowing what the right hand is doing", for even as the conscious mind may not grasp it, the intelligent body that is comprised of the electromagnetic forces of the DNA fields knows everything that is going on in the body. But there is one more aspect that We want you to know and appreciate. And that is that the electromagnetic fields of your intelligent body (which are beginning to be measured by scientists) allow you to focus that energy where you will - choose to. And so, as you feel discomfort in your belly and focus on that area, you will notice a magnification of the discomfort. That is because the fields, when fed with consciousness will enlarge, magnify, amplify the signals, much like when electricity is pumped through an amplifier. The sound signal increases dramatically. And so, the energy of consciousness interacts with the electromagnetic fields of the intelligent body to amplify whatever is focused upon. Now how does this information assist you in your day-to-day activities? The first manner in which it can help is to let you know that each moment you focus on discomforts, disease, pain, suffering in your body, you are amplifying those signals and the pain or disease becomes worse. On the other hand, each time you focus on the beauty, on the healing, on the gracefulness and ease the body feels, the greater those characteristics become. So, be astute as to what you do with your attention. Your smart body will know and take care of the physical body better if you recognize and appreciate the beating of your heart, the flawless skin, the efficient digestions, the continuous intake of air. Feel these aspects of your body, know they are well tended. And do not add your consciousness to those aspects of your physicality that you do not want to magnify. As this is practiced, you will gradually become more aware of your well-being and your intelligent electro-magnetic body will be better able to correct any diseases or pain when they are no longer fed. This is all.

Amplify the Good

19

Allow Spirit to Take Care of You

Fill your heart with joy. Today and all days. For you should already know there is no other way of Being that Creative God Source would have you be. Joyful, in the knowledge that you are an expression of the Divine Creator. Joyful in the knowing that Creative Source resides within you. Joyful because you have the gifts of Source all around you for the asking. Joyful because your bodies take such good care to nurture and support your spirit. Joyful as you feel the merge with your Higher Self each day. Joyful because you are always well-cared for as you allow it.

Be patient with yourself. It is only in the practice lifetime after lifetime that the ability to release to a form of acceptance truly becomes refined. As it was stated, this is the year of allowing … Please allow Us to care for you, to immerse you in the well-waters of well-being and please trust Us, that we will not fail you. I stand with you in all you do, today and all days. For I, Christ, am only a part of the essence that has come to be You. Together we share creation. Together we will make the year of allowing peaceful, joyful and a true manifestation of the power of immeasurable love.

20

Move On

There has been much drama in your past. It is easy for you and many to slip into the victim mentality. This is a particularly unwise and unpleasant path, for it is self-sustaining. The more you pity yourself, see yourself as harmed, or blame those around you, the greater the harm to you will be. For it is as the Law of Attraction teaches...that which you think becomes your reality. And also the stated law of physics - for every action there is an equal and opposite reaction. The harder you push to seek justice, uncover wrongdoing or pin blame on others the greater the "push-back" onto self. If, on the other hand, you focus on forgetting negative actions against you, on forward movement and building or re-building your life, your wealth, your happiness, the easier it will be for you. For example, as you move toward adjusting your lifestyle for your age and your health, you can assess your needs, adapt your expectations and merely wait, with trust and appreciation, that your needs will be met. Relax into the knowing. Relax into understanding you DO NOT NEED to push for what you desire. The Universe is delivering it to your front door, as you stand breaking open your mailbox. Stop doing those things that do not serve you. Let the "chips' fall where they may. It truly will be a brighter day if you keep your eyes open rather than closed to the abundance that is already about you.

Be at peace. Know your Spiritual guides and angelic Beings are with you to hold you up as you move forward toward your true reason for being in this time and place. Do not get derailed, for all of my Children have important parts to play in the Eternity game.

Let it be. Move on. Proof is unnecessary. Be joyful at what remains with you that allows so much more satisfaction than before. Look into the New energy and understand it is your love, not resentment or victimized mindset, that will powerfully shape your future and that of Mother Gaia. Understand so much does not matter. So much of what you spend your time on. You would be better served by sitting in meditation until you cannot help from jumping up to attend to a task. That is all that is needed. This is what you needed to know today and all days. Go in peace and know my love is with you, always, and I want only joy and prosperity for my children. Rest quietly. Enjoy your 'free' time - the time free of actions.

21

Be Vigilant with Your Thoughts

As you move closer to the vibration that is characteristic of your Higher Self, you manifest that which you think about more quickly. Now there are some of you who are moving closer to that vibration, but, be mindful that you still have a distance yet to go. For this reason you are learning slowly the vast difference between being in a positive place and how dramatically that contrasts with being in a negative mindset, even for a few minutes, even as pretending or acting, even as remembering or complaining, these vibrations pull you down and defeat your purposes. This will attract more of the like and reflect back to you exactly where your mindset exists. So, I say to you, keep the fires of vigilance burning so that you don't let yourself be drawn into the negative realms of magnetism. Rather, stay positive, feel the power of love and craft only the beautiful products of your creations. In all you do, bless your work, your manifestations no matter how small. For much like a proud little child with a work of his/her own doing, you will soon learn to build bigger and better creations. With unmeasurable love, we send you Our aid.

Fleeting Moments of Love

22

Feel the Moments of Love

You have profound experiences when you begin to feel the intensity of the flowing well of love that bathes you at all times. Little does that even come close to reaching the true depth and intensity of that existing energy of which you are made. Many of you on Earth at this time obtain glimpses of this love occasionally as a mother holds her babe, a father tends his son or a couple reaches brief climax together. These moments are fleeting. These moments are rare. And yet, these moments uncover the fabric of which All is made. It is only a brief second when you are immersed in your feelings of love that you get a fleeting view of the fabric of the Universe. And so, My Children, it is with this in your minds, that I ask you to keep your eyes open wider, open longer. For each time you view this excruciatingly beautiful fabric of love, the less time you will choose to be without love.

23

Acknowledge Source Accompanies You

Play not in the realms of the physical such that you miss the bliss of the non-physical. For all your days are spent with cognitive tasks, focusing on a list of chores and even lists of "fun" things as though they also are milestones which need be accomplished in specific time periods. Take more of your day, your hours, your minutes to dwell not in the physical place only, but merge and be mindful of the spiritual within you at all times. It is much like carrying a baby on your back. As such, you proceed through your day unmindful of the baby. As the baby hungers you ignore it until its cries become uncomfortable. As you wear your baby, you are oblivious to its wants and how to keep it safe. As you sit in a chair you crush it. As you lean against a wall it is pressed. As you eat and drink, the baby becomes more hungry and thirsty. As this allows you to understand better that spirit / God/ Christ /Creative Source is always with you. You may choose to be oblivious to its presence and the potential for reciprocal love. Yet, like with a baby, a few moments of nurture brings nutrition and strength; avoidance of harmful practices protects the essence and through becoming aware of Spirit you can develop the most loving shared relationship like that of a mother and a baby.

So I ask that each day, find some time to sit quietly or discover your own way of becoming cognizant of the Spirit within you. As you move through your day be aware you are sharing everything that occurs with Spirit. When good approaches, welcome it with open arms and give some credit to the Spirit working from within. As I say in many ways, when you learn to acknowledge Who You Are and become practiced in recognizing the brilliance of the merge of our physical body with the essence of Spirit with you, you will only then begin to experience the sweetness of life that way that Creative Source intended. Do not be fooled by those who would torment you with promises of hell and threats of retribution at a final judgement Day.

For you have already been judged. Judged as magnificent, worthy Beings of All Love and judged as the perfection that is created by the Perfect Creator.

Know you are loved beyond measure. Act like it. Trust it. Know that love is the power of your life and you, only you, Dear Ones, can choose how you use that power. This is All.

24

Knock Only

There is a difference between knocking on a door, pushing on a door and knocking a door down. Be careful which of these choices you focus on. For the ease and grace that is there for the asking will allow doors to be opened for you with a mere knock. If you choose to push a bit, that is your choice for you have free will to select and focus on anything you want. I invite you, Children, not to break doors down. If the persons on the other side don't willingly and joyfully grant you access, there is foreboding. If the door is now broken, there are reparations to be made, time involved in the repairs and lessened goodwill toward all.

So, Dear Ones, I suggest, invite you, to consider going only where you are wanted and when you are wanted. If you knock on a door and it is not opened for you....wait a period of time and knock again. It should take no pushing or breaking it down if it is on the path your soul has defined with you when you were unaware in this consciousness. Go always and all ways with ease and grace. Think about this message and let it guide you.

25

Practice Love

The heart of a child is quite small in size. And yet it beats fast and hard to push the blood through young arteries and veins. The heart of an elder is small too, yet it beats slowly, less powerfully but sends blood to and through a much larger body. So this is with love. As love is young and new and fresh, it is ripe with anticipation. The love comes fast as the heart beats quickly in young love. As love matures, there are times of rapid beats, times when love seems to miss a step or beat, and other times, quiet times, the love is peaceful and quiescent. All of these stages and cycles lead to a maturation of love. It is never stagnant; like the blood, love moves continuously, allowing the body to experience the fresh blood in every tissue with each heartbeat. As the body ages, the love becomes easier. The heart does not need to beat as hard or as rapidly to keep blood flowing through the body of the elder. It knows its path. It fills the chambers. It reaches all cells with the deftness of practice. And, as one becomes more practiced at feeling love, showing love and living in a pool surrounded by love, the easier it becomes. With practice, love will also improve. The more practiced one becomes at expressing love - all forms - all the continuously changing forms, the easier and better the love comes to all. Understand that your heart beat IS love; your blood, the sustenance of life. So as you nurture your heart, hear its calls, and respond to its contractions you will enable the love in your life to come readily to you and be expressed easily to all of those you touch.

26

Abolish Guilt

Be. Be who it is you really Are. Be gentle. Be patient. Be kind. Be first, gentle with yourself. For if you are not gentle and kind and patient with self, then there is no chance, no opportunity for the self to know how to extend those blessings to others. For in the working mind, as you go about your day it is the way that many of My Children chastise themselves. As you continue to self-abuse through your thoughts you begin to believe that you are not worthy of love, that you can be better, do better. Then allowing the guilt to come and direct your selves even farther from the path you have chosen for yourselves. This snowballs and rolls you in an uncontrolled direction where it becomes harder and harder to find your original intent. I urge you to abolish guilt first. For with any behaviors that are driven by guilt there is accompanying resentment and self-hatred. Realize first that you owe no one your life, or your time, only your love. Realize next that anything you do out of guilt will come around to sustain those feelings. And realize third, that it is far better never to do anything that you know, in advance, will produce feelings of guilt with which you force yourselves to live.

Again, throw away guilt from all aspects of your life. Guilt about who you haven't become, what you have or have not done, how you have been in relationships, how you use your life. Guilt serves no purpose for you. It is but a means by which others control you. Abolish guilt from your life and then you will have greater freedom. And in that freedom you can choose to be gentle, be kind, be patient. These are who you Be. You are a holy expression of the love of God. You are the breath of life in this Universe. You are a magnificent Being, part God-Source, part human. Be all of these, as you were Created. There is no room or cause or need to be guilty for who you Are.

27

Whispers of God

The pineal is indeed a portal. For most, but not all, there is the tendency to allow the Spirit of God-Source and non- physical entities to flow through the veil and into human consciousness. The ability has always been with humans to a greater or lesser extent. In the old days before writing was common-place there was the enhanced ability to hear and perceive language in the silence of one's perceptual field. This ability diminished over time. But in those days there was little to discriminate the whispers of God-Source from intuition from thoughts arising in one's neighbors. With the intense focus on physical means of communication such as writing, TV, radio, printed text, there is a knowledge of the very discrete sources of material. There has been little focus, outside of meditative practices, on the ability to focus on the words that come across the veil through the pineal. Edgar Cayce is now the best known channel in the western world, but it was only because he lay "sleeping" during the transmission that people have accepted the mystery and to some extent the veracity of the process of channeling. As the new energy infiltrates into your Gaia and more people put out the intention to commune with Spirit, this ability will be refound.

The pineal needs to be clear of crust - calcification to be a clear portal. The vegetables and oils of your diet, if eaten in properly large amounts will lessen the accumulation of crust. For those who wish to remain open the absence or limiting of dairy, heavy meats is called for; and sugars should be avoided. This will allow the pineal to continue to function and become more proficient with practice. Listen, then, Children, to the quick, quiet whispers that come to you at the most unexpected time. Learn to discriminate those messages from those delivered to you by your thoughts and the world about you. Sit quietly in meditative practice and that may assist many. Above all, know that your own thoughts are often a mixture of divine messaging and that which you choose to attend to with your free choice and focus. Be peaceful about this, for those whispers will always communicate the unmeasurable love that is here for you.

Be peaceful

28

Move Forward

There will be a small war soon. Small in that those who perpetrate
the devastation are a few in number. Not small in the impact their
methods of choice will have globally. This is a time of patience.
This is a time of choice. As the world receives this blow, there are
individuals who have been born specifically to endure this. This
does not dampen the grief that will be felt. It does not minimize
the loss. The words of comfort that I share with you, Children, are
few but of great importance. Do not steep in the bitterness for that
will only prolong and enlarge the negative impact. Move forward
in your choices quickly and know that things will not be the same
as before. Accept all around you with love and compassion. There
are those who will have a great variety of needs. Do not be fearful
of meeting those needs. And, finally, trust. Trust in the kindness
of Spirit for there will be a brilliant future for humanity yet. It is
already done.

29

Trust Positive Intentions

There are no small things. Every act, each thought, each word is a weight that falls upon the Earth's record, the Earth's ears and changes the relationship between humanity and Mother Gaia. I say to you that all good intentions are real, quite in contrast to the statements made by clergy that the "road to Hell is paved with good intentions"! That is an untruth for, in all things, your vibration transmits your intentions and those can be and are read by the Earth and transmitted to change the Universe. So, you see, good intentions are important regardless of how they are read by others. Pure positive intentions such as those of peace and harmony, kindness and gentle soothing ARE interpreted accurately by Gaia. Keep your faith that you are acknowledged for your being and that Being Who You Really Are converges with the intentions of the very wise and benevolent Universe. In this you may trust. So, for the record, all good comes from good intentions – those felt from the heart, but not necessarily seen by your eyes. Be peaceful in the knowing that good intentions are never overlooked by Spirit. And so it is.

30

Spiritual Merging

The Words of Spirit flow freely. They are hovering in the air, whispered in your ear, there to reach for and grasp. The Words of Spirit are free to every person who asks to receive and who takes the time to practice receiving these Words in this new energy. All are prepared with the skills and physical characteristics that permit receiving the Words of Spirit. Many have never opened these gifts, others have allowed for short periods but often drawn away due to focus on some drama in their life or another. And then there are a few - and there need not be many who seek the Words of Spirit, who have learned to trust, who feel the love and emotions with the messages and are willing to practice receiving. Not always will this persevere. The Words of Spirit are uncanny in that often, just as they are relevant to the receiver, they also pertain to the many. For an example, as Words come through to warn an individual of a potential for a bicycle accident in their real life, the story can also be a figurative story to direct the many on how to avoid accidents that may harm them in the spiritual realm. For there is a 3rd language... the language of love that is felt, not spoken; that is more real and Universal than the written text and endures in the records of time on Earth. This is being prepared, now, as this moon hovers over the world.

The new energy uses Luna to translate and transmit in the language of love the Creative Source's universal communication of benevolence. The cold, the snow, the rain, the floods all work together to enhance the circles of love that dwell in all the communities and give opportunity to those who wish to migrate to a different form to manifest their exit from the Earth body. They will most probably return in a new state of Being in the Earth time/space to come as interested in more of the spiritual merging than they expressed in the life they exited. It is all part of the plan with which humans, in their magnificence and glory express the new and deserved manifestations they have so concertedly put into place. The love is palpable and will continue to shed more light on the planet as the dark disappears and is cleared. Rejoice. Be joyful for this is a beautiful time in your life cycles. Appreciate that you are All the One that has chosen to bring in this new era and new energy. And so it is.

The Dark Dissipates

31

Direct The Energy

We are all in this together. The energy that is 'All That Is' is the same energy that powers you, your parents and grandparents that have passed and the most hated rulers in the world. That energy is maleable and can be shaped and stretched, can be used for good or less than good. All of this is determined by your free choice. Your "mind" my Dear Ones is a most powerful tool. It is a tool that you were gifted with in the early days of your Creation. You have not all used the tool of your conscious mind as well as you could have, and so, like an unused muscle, your minds have become weak. Now, you are being given a gift that will enhance your ability to revisit how you use your conscious mind. In the new energy that is being delivered to you now, there is a sharpening edge, a creative addition, an intuitive power that will, if you choose to accept it, allow your conscious mind to take you places you have not been before. You may now learn quickly of the true power of your conscious thought for it will make your lives easier, your world more peaceful and your joy, uninhibited. This new energy must be directed or it will lead to discomfort and unrest. It is the same as the energy in your belly as you wake. Grab it, direct it according to your will, and, most importantly, be thankful for it. It is a gift, much deserved, that will allow you to proceed to your next level of Being. You are loved beyond measure and this new energy, turned to joy and Light is just one more expression of the Creator's unending love for you. So it is.

32

Choose

You already know much of what you need to know. I urge you now to think more clearly than ever before and choose your path, your thoughts and your words, based on what you know. You are blessed. Use it.

33

Breath of Ecstasy

There are cases in every culture on Earth where individual humans have had the spiritual experience of breath of ecstasy. This state of existence has been long sought after because of the bliss and euphoria that communion with our Higher Self in God Source provides. In some religious practices this state has been achieved through total cleansing of the thoughtful mind allowing Spirit to access conscious awareness. In other cultures the state has been sought after and achieved after firm and lengthy periods of focusing on the disciplined body thus attenuating other conscious thought, and allowing bliss or nirvana to occur. Still other practices have included prayer. Prayer in the continuous breath and repetition of chants in every minute for extended times. It matters little what the chant is but that rhythmic breathing paired with calming the thoughtful mind is sufficient to invite such a state as breath of ecstasy. There is little known about the origins in humans of these practices but I tell you they have all been experienced by your "religious" and non-religious as well. Learn the breath of ecstasy, yes, by breathing deeply and rhythmically as you first wake up in the morning. The blissful state will be retained longer with each practice. Soon you will be able to create it at will. Do this if you choose to be at one with your Higher Being.

For God Source is in all things and movement is the characteristic trait of Source Energy. As such, the Creative Source exists in the air you breathe and its movement through you is empowering and blissful. Use this tool now, so that you may have it readily at hand when it is needed and that you may teach your friends and others on Earth this valuable tool that connects each of my Children to Spirit merely by using the gift of breath to produce ecstasy. Believe this and then experience it. This is yet another gift due to the unmeasurable love that surrounds you from Source Energy.

34

Universal Motion

There is no space between Us. For as Spirit envelops All That Is, the Creative Source permeates and continually moves through all of creation. It is in this constant motion that the Universe, as you know it, resides. For the sun moves, the moons move around moving planets and your atoms, even those in your body continually move. As movement is the nature of Universal law, all things must stay in constant flux. The needs, the wants, the prayers, the thoughts, the actions are all reflections of this principle.

However, differences exist in the rate of movement. The vibratory nature of matter and Spirit determines the shift, the magnitude and the ease. Humans vibrate at markedly variant rates and those that vibrate higher add considerably more flux to the system. Those that vibrate at the lower rates tend to be stagnant, unchanging and set in their ways. They look not for newness, change or to alter themselves or their world in any way. I ask now, at this time on Earth that those who are accustomed to movement and change be at the sides of those who find it much more difficult. For now, all things on Earth will be in continuous motion for a time. It will be those who vibrate at lower rates who will have most difficulty.

Take their hands, let them know they are not alone and there is help for the asking. Go now, in kindness and discover those among you who are in such a place. Let them know it is all right and that they will yet be able to discover their own state of well-being. All on Earth is blessed. Want only what you would have for All. You are loved beyond measure. It can only grow.

35

Divine Spark

I am old. I am ageless by all standards. I have been with you on earth in many physical forms - both man and woman and, yes, sometimes of undetermined sex.My time in the physical was spent in many lifetimes in service to others. In the life when I was known as Jesus, to you, and Jeshua to my friends, I serviced those around me by my modeling the power and calm and magnificence of the God within all of you. But at that time humanity was so beaten down, so saddened by their conditions of life and so far removed from their Higher Selves, they could not imagine that they too, were Sons and Daughters of God. It is truth. In each Divine descendent of the Creative Source lies the same cord, spark, fire of Divinity. You are now as I was in the body. You now are close enough to the Light to seek and find the power within you that was in me. I am here today and all days to urge you on, to blend your Higher Self and your physical bodies. There is only All That Is. There is only one Universal energy stream that arises from the God Source. Realize that you are emanations from and of that Source. You will return, merge, and cycle again and again through many temporary houses or bodies. But know, too, that there will be periods of time when you are like me now. Fully present in everything and everyone, but not corporeal. I am merged with the Universal energy stream not as an individual but as the Spiritual energy, the Creative energy, the same Divinity that runs through you. It is the proper time in this new energy to stand tall, follow your heart and know through to your core, that you are Sons and Daughters of God. And, you can do, be, or have everything I did and was and more. Go being blessed in the glorious sunlight of your emergence into who you know you are.

Light up each Dawn

36

Power of Intent

One day at a time. This is a common saying but not many of you know the origins of this saying. It was, in another Era, the religious/spiritual principle that all were taught from childhood. It was the most sincere expression of trust in Universal benevolence and the creative power of Source Energy. This adage combined with simple pure intention is how other races in other times flourished. For they knew far better, then, how to rely on synchronicities, on their intuition, to guide their thoughts and deeds. By releasing all concerns and worries of what was to be tomorrow, they focused only on what was in front of them today. They lived with pure intention, and, therefore freedom to choose DAILY what they wanted. And, with the practice, day after day, since childhood, those races were able to listen to Spirit, create great technologies, solve all problems and most importantly, create communities of love and harmony. No one worried about food or resources, so there was no reason to take it from another. No one needed more in the future than that which was constantly being provided, so there was no need for war. And, in the knowing that intent had power to create, to harm, to renew - there was the learning to direct intention in a focused and constructive creative way.

I ask that those of you for whom this sounds like an attractive way to Be, begin taking things day by day, one day at a time, one hour, one minute at a time. For the now is your power point. It is the intention in the now that brings about your next now. And this is the way it always has been. Trust then, that the God that is All That Is hears and knows your intent in every second of every day and coordinates the Universe to deliver. So be confident. Do your experiments and learn how you can be, have and do what you choose, what pleases you, with direct awareness of putting forth your intent. This is how it always has been, and how it will always be on earth. There is only one caveat I offer to you. The power of loving intentions far out-weighs the power of hatred, vengeance, cruelty, control over others. So, unless you choose to have negative creations snowball out-of-control in your life and the lives of others, take great care to impose loving, kind, compassionate intentions on this world that you create. Love all. Trust the Source of All. And you will feel, see and realize peace and harmony in every second of every day. Much love is with you to guide you, as you ask.

37

Change

There is change all about you, yet you do not see it. Each day is different for nature never repeats a cycle exactly in the same way. All manner of animals move about, change their world in nature. Each body on the earth looses cells and replaces cells each day. All of this change is a slow process, yet all of this you do not realize is taking you to a different place of Being. If you choose to write daily, the muscles in your hand become stronger. If you eat large amounts of food, your stomach expands. And as you choose your daily behaviors your body, your environment, and your awareness and expectations change as well.

And so why do I tell you this at this time?

For while you cannot observe it, you have always been immersed in a changing world. I tell you now that you may begin to observe change in all that is around you and in your conscious state of awareness. It really is no different from what has always been. The only differences are that the changes come faster and are often observable to you, your eyes, your bodies, your senses. But, remember that change has always been a part of your existence. So, do not be afraid of rapid change. Just know that it is taking you where you choose to be in a much faster way than before. Embrace it like you would grab and hold the bars on a roller-coaster ride. We are with you. The real you will always live on. We are here to assist and want to deliver to you in ways that you can feel our unmeasurable love for you. Go, peacefully, and know you are love.

38

Love is Energy

It is time for the answers to come to you and many about the reality that you cannot see. There are, there will be ways to begin to see the energy that makes up your planet and that which drifts through your Universe. Your astro-physicists are already viewing your cosmos through many types of filters. These filters have enabled them to see a small amount of energy in the form of high energy emitting particles and various wavelengths of light. Soon, so keep your awareness on the astro-physicists, they will announce an unusual filter that allows the envisioning of the energy masses that congeal to form your physical world. Many will not know what this is. The same technology can be used to watch the surges and fluidity of the energy you call love. With these filtering devices you will be able to measure, to a limited extent, a flow of visually detected energy that correlates with streaming love. Once this is accepted by the younger ones on Earth there will be a conscious channeling of love to all parts of your planet that have been deprived. This will begin a new era of understanding that love energy is a real force in your world and that it can be used for many purposes. Creating peace, healing, calming and congealing other energies into matter. Those who know of this already must feel their calling to teach those who want to know. This will be forming soon. Be aware of your calling for you are in the right place at the right time to share such knowledge. And so it is.

Filters - Seeing the Energy

39

Refinement

Refinement will come as you move farther into this new energy. Your intentions will hold more sway, you will begin to see how you are influencing your world, the people around you, and the consequences of your thoughts and actions. Be not afraid of this power, for some of you have used it in your past and become shocked that your thoughts ruled your environment. Now, Children, you know some of the rules. Play nicely in the sandbox with your friends. Kindness, graciousness and empathy will lead you to envision only good for yourself and those around you, especially your loved ones. Do not worry about your family, your children. Rather, spend your thought time in clear envisioning of how you want them to be happy, no matter what it takes. Send streaming love and feel it move from your heart to theirs. Love all that is about you for the power of love pulls the strings that bring things together in the right place at the right time. Know, My Dears, that all of this is by plan. Not so hardwired that it is known what will happen, but hardwired to give the maximum flexibility to the software programs of your lives. As you move into this new energy, many of you will allow greater knowledge to flow, and with that knowledge, you will begin to practice these things - kind thoughts, words and deeds, allowance and acceptance of all that is good and the manifestation of that which you choose. With continued practices there comes refinement as you learn what this new energy will translate and what it will not. Be open, continue to experiment and learn. And then move your light into the world so that others may learn, too. Be joyful, for you are on the brink of creating the "Golden Age" in your lifetimes. I see from where I Am the potentials for the movement of Creation outward. This is the grandest interpolation of all consciousness. Be glad with this, for you chose to be here for the now that you are experiencing with All That Is. It could have turned out much different, but for the love each of you has shown to the other. Your hardships are done, if you choose. Your new self is being created by You. And the All That Is will benefit by your design. There is much love for you and always.

40

Enrich Life

Art is life. Life is Art. The greater your appreciation for the art that exists around you, every piece of nature, cloud in the sky, chair and table, the richer your life will be. Look around you at the magnificent fabrics that touch your body, frame your windows, lay on your floor. Each of these is a form of art with an artist who created and other 'artists' who designed to place it in your reach.

Most of humanity works with some form of art enriching their lives. There are the obvious professions that include musicians, painters, and sculptors, architects, fashion designers and display artists. But art is an ever present component of every day. The china on your table, the images on your coffee cups, the design of a tea pot. Art is an expression of the Divine within you and in others. In this way, through connecting with the beauty, individual styles and the nuances of that which surrounds you, you may derive a greater appreciation and therefore a greater richness of your life. As you do this, as in many other tools I have given you, there will come a time that you, too, see only art in your life. The way colors, events, people and opportunities align can be called nothing less than art. And in this mindset, this is what is referred to as Spiritual vision - all that you see and partake of is elegant and beautiful and woven together in a massive spiritual blanket. As you begin to see the patterns emerge, you will be in awe at the Mastery behind the plan to Create this Art of your Life.

Life is Art

41

God Consciousness

There are no thoughts that go unwatched. For many of you think thoughts are private and belong only to you. But, Dear Children, this is not the case. For all thoughts are part of a constant stream of energy. Energy flowing from us to you, or from you to us, or from you to others. As I am before you now, sending these thoughts one word at a time, your thoughts are also read and heard by us, but multidimensionally and without the restrictions of time. I call upon you all to monitor your thoughts, to think and offer, in the beginning, more positive thoughts than negative ones. As you do this, you will begin to feel calmer, more joyful and more at ease with who you are and where you are in your life. As you begin to feel better, more thoughts that you offer will naturally become happy, joyful, optimistic. It is a cycle. And the same cycle works also for negative thoughts. And you ask how to tell the difference? Are there neutral thoughts? And yes, there are neutral thoughts that act like roadblocks and keep you where you are. The positive thoughts are those that make you feel better and nudge you to move farther forward on your path. The negative thoughts fill you with fear, hate, jealousy, vengeance, and cunning. These thoughts take you on a detour - how far and long you remain on that detour is up to you.

Stay calm. Think of things that you would like to share with Spirit. For every thought you think is offered to us. It is watched, and heard and monitored without judgment. So know this Dear Ones, and, again, choose who and what you want to express at this time in your Planet's evolution into the New Energy. You are loved beyond measure no matter how you choose, for you are a part of the eternal stream of consciousness you call "God".

42

Transformative Power

You need to grow. All of my children will benefit from taking the next step. I am not saying that you are not mature. I only tell you that, like a mother talking with her 6 yr old, she knows that he will eventually grow into a man. So it is with Spiritual growth. We see you and feel you and know that you will grow into magnificent Spiritual beings who coexist quite consciously in your human bodies. You will grow into more expansive Beings by allowing your Higher Self and Creative Source to move into your conscious awareness and guide you. You will grow away from using your brain to evaluate and make each choice for you. You will grow into your heart and receive guidance from your Higher Self to keep you on the path you choose. Yes, it is the right time.

Please be cognizant that this new energy is transformative. It will take you where you want to go much faster and more directly than the old energy. So, quietly decide who you are and who you want to be, how you want to continue to grow into your skin from a Spiritual point of Being. And then trust it will be so. For you are powerful Beings and the Universe awaits your decisions so that it may arrange All That Is to meet your desires/commands. It is with great love this is done for you, unto you. Like a mother who helps her son grow by daily feeding him fresh and nourishing food.

43

Two Homes

One is never consciously aware that death is near. And this is by design for you would live that time differently in the knowing. However, your Higher Self and Innate Intelligent body do know, for all aspects of You plan, and that plan often corresponds to the plan you laid forth before you came into this physical body.

Live each day as if your death were near. This will provide opportunity to feel the beauty around you. It will allow you to appreciate Mother Gaia in a different way from just tromping on her shell. But most of all, it will help you to realize the love and attachments you have to the others in your life. You are not in this time and place alone. You have come into clusters of/or soul groups to which many of you have been attached for eons. These soul groups, although not singular in and of themselves, comprise entities to which you are connected. As you take leave from your body for a short time before renewing, you will feel like you are cutting off a finger or toes. This feeling of not being whole or missing something is because of the tight connections that you have with those with whom you love. I tell you now, you are all connected - all part of the single Creative Source and energy that emanates from Creator. In the passing from physical to non-physical there is great joy and peace and a reception for another coming home. And in that state, there is still the great love to be with those other parts of you in the physical. This love, this longing is part of what impels you to return to the Earth and your soul group. For you see you really do have two homes. Both of these have their unique beauty and blessings.

44

Offer the State of Prayer

There is a battle being fought now. Much as you, Dear Children, would prefer to hide your eyes, you will benefit by not. Rather, know this battle must be fought. It is the battle that will define humankind for the next Era of life on this planet. And know, Children, you can, as you choose, contribute. If you choose to do nothing and know nothing and acknowledge nothing, that, be as it may, is sufficient. For in that, the betterment of your society will still emerge. If, however, you choose to participate you have many ways that are effective. Pray. Pray for peace on Earth especially in the danger zones. Send love to those who need to feel that love - both those opened up to dark, and those who walk in the Light. Send conscious intent with your breath for the most beneficial outcome. As you do these things, repeatedly, the Earth will transmit your vibration and assist in the acceleration of peaceful existence on Earth. You can choose to have a role - a minor role as a unit - but a major role if many of you choose to pray, together or alone. Choose to send compassionate love to those who are wounded, lost, afraid and hurting - not only in the battle zones but throughout your beautiful Earth. It does little good for you to sequester your thoughts and focus your energies on the mundane activities of your lives. Yes, please cook, clean, work and toil in your gardens, but do so in the state of joyous prayer, sublime peace and happiness. For in offering that state - which also IS a Prayer, to All That Is - you make the largest mark you can on this Earth. And, Dear Ones, this is the time, the best point in time for that choice.

So disallow hatred, resentment, jealousy and petty discontents from your awareness. Focus only on that which is peaceful, in harmonious existence around you and on the general well-being and beauty of your Planet, Mother Gaia.

However you choose to Be, choose. Choose it now, actively, and with deep existence. This is the way forward into the new energy, where everything, every thought, every act will have a much faster vibration and a more rapid manifestation. So, I urge you, choose wisely, for you are learning to manifest even if you choose to learn "the hard way". Go in the knowing that you are loved beyond measure. Know it, show it, share it for if not you, then who?

Accelerate Peace

45

Choose Wisely

All That I AM, you know. For in the physical, you do not remember Who I Am, but in the non-physical you are fully conscious and aware that you Are part of Me. For we flow together through time, through what you think of as space. Yes, we flow and merge with the beautiful formations of your galaxies and the planets and suns as they birth and also die, or recycle their energy to other physicalities. You are a part of the loving God Source as it flows continually. It is true that you are eternal, no matter what choices you make. Only a part - a tiny fragment of All that is you is now "in your body". Most of You continues to flow and ebb, merge and separate from the Creative Source that is All That Is. Your continuation in the physical, even though it may make up many lifetimes, for you is but a moment in the eternalness of Source. Yes, your choices make a difference in each day, each Era, so choose wisely. Choose for your own benefit and for the Highest Good. As the Universal consciousness knows both, this choice can never fail you, even if appearances fool you for a short time. I know that there are matters at hand where it appears that the world is left without love, peace or sanity. Know, release yourself to the trusting, that Creative Source, with your loving choices, is preparing yet a better world for you to continue your jaunts in the excitement, the bliss, the sensory delights of physicality on Earth. Know this is just one more manifestation of the Eternal and unmeasurable love that Creative Source or God holds for you. Rest easily, Dear Ones. There is nothing to fear.

46

Focus

Focus. Focus your time on those around you. As you learn to do this you will clearly see that this action facilitates the synchronicities of your life. And theirs. All around you are things to tend to, calls to make, purchases and errands to run. But how many times have you focused your attention on another to Be with them, talk to them and serve their needs? I ask that you try this for one week. You will be astounded at the power of co-creation and they may suspect your methods - so on track they are. Give this your focus. Each day for 7 days. Think about that person early in the day, reach out, talk, serve them and most importantly feel love in your heart for them. They can be friend, family or foe. They will all respond to your efforts with renewed hope and gratitude. Be this way and learn how to teach by your example. One day at a time.

47

Believe

As you know things to be, that is how they will be. As in the words of other teachers, belief is the prime mover especially when combined with love and intent. You think of love only as a feeling. This is partly true because of the way you experience or feel it. It is far more than a feeling but the yarn by which the galaxies and universes are woven together. I have said before, the Universe is powered by love and this is as accurate a statement whether you are discussing religion, psychology or physics. In all of these forums, love - and there will be better words in time to describe love, is the force - an actual force like gravity that moves, pushes, pulls, inspires and shapes your world. I say to you now, believe and it will be so. Apply loving trust to your belief and it will be so, sooner. Apply unwavering faith and pure kind intention and it will emerge in far better form than you, alone, could ever plan. Know there is a cadre of spiritual beings who, if you ask, assist you in all things. They will help you - all you need to do is believe they are at your side, as I am. In most days, it is clear there are forces at work in your lives. Be sure this is no accident. Ask for the proof. Be not surprised when it arrives. You are loved always. And, so it is.

48

Love is Reciprocated

The love of a pet. The pet - whether it be dog, cat, rabbit, goat or rodent, is a very immersive experience and good for the animal, the person and good for Earth's energy enrichment. The bond that grows is because the animal becomes totally dependent on the person for their well-being - their food, drink, shelter, warmth and their exposure to others than their self. The energy of love that the animal develops is different from human love but surely as intense. As the person comes back to join their pet, there is an outflowing of love that surely is tangible and felt equally between the person and the pet. This is something all pet owners have experienced.

In the same way is the difference between the love of Creative Source for each human and each human who knows Creative Source. When they come together, there is an outpouring of a highly dynamic and irresistible love that is felt on both sides. Make no mistake this joining has been happening for millennium. Your Catholic nuns know the flow, your ascetics in India feel the tangible euphoria, the monks in all cultures work and discover this and it makes their lives better.

Toni Page

This also holds true for Creator on the other side. When the love flows it is mutual and both sides experience the beauty of the Way. I guide you, Children, to learn and then practice feelings of love for your God, your Creator. And when you do, know that love is magnified and reciprocated. Do this daily if you can. The communion with Spirit will, like loving a pet, become so tangible you will be unable to conceptualize living without it. And so, this may appear overly simple to many. I urge you to give God no less love than you give your pet.

New Horizons

49

Set the Tone

Fresh and clean is the new day. Each day that you awake with a clean, fresh, new mind - one not bogged down in worry for the future or regret of the past - is a chance to reroute your path. As you wake your slate has been wiped 'clean'. In the first few minutes of breathing life into the new day, the tone is set. If you rise and you immediately focus your thoughts on aches and pains your whole day will be one of aches and pains. If you greet the morning, the sun, the birdsong with a feeling of appreciation, gentleness and welcome, your entire day will be an invitation to Spirit to bring you more. Please test this for yourself. Alas, it is difficult not to let the worries creep into your mind, but you can and have done it on many occasions. Wake with the will to let only pleasantness and kindness and love permeate your mind. Soon, it will flood your life. Think not of difficulty parking, rather know a place is beckoning you. Think not of paying bills, but of spreading the good and abundance and joy of prosperity as widely as you can. Think not of danger in your activities and travels, but think of the adventure and laughter and awe new horizons bring you. Do this as often as you can, for it is in setting the tone for the day that strides are made each minute into your future. So choose your thoughts, each morning as the new, fresh and clear day begins.

50

Love is Energy

You are complete in the now. There is no missing piece - no separate block or person or trait that will make you whole. Your existence is and has always been a complete energy form that is eternal. Nothing needs to be added for you are whole as you are. Yes, you change your forms of expression from the time of birth, throughout childhood and as adults who age...and again in recycling the spirit through death and rebirth. You change form, names, skin texture and color but you do not require anything, either from without or within because you are whole - complete as you are. You lack nothing. You have within your essence everything you need to do, and be, and have anything you choose. Know it in your Being. There is nothing you can strive for that does not already exist within you. Find it, ask Me, Spirit to assist you. Please, never feel less than whole or incomplete. You are a work of God Source who leaves nothing unfinished. Know you are loved as you Are. Now and always. Amen.

51

Grow

There is growth. There is growth all around you in the leaves, the trees, the new life forms that enjoy your lakes. The flowers are beginning their growth too. There is life - wherever there is growth - and death where there is stagnation. This, too, is a season for personal and spiritual growth. One needs to grow toward Beings of Light and away from base beings who are incarnate. One needs to grow toward healthy habits and using one's acquired wisdom and not fall back on habits that no longer serve the Highest Good. All this is what you already know. We invite you to ponder this. Whether you choose to stagnate in a repetitive series of motions and emotions, or whether to choose a new life, a new reality and move to it with faith and trust that you, in your Higher wisdom have designed this plan well and with the greatest love. Be in peace. Choose. And be joyful in your new life.

52

Gaia Sees

Today is a catalytic day. You have already seen the birds - geese, the ducks attending to the different energy today. There will be great changes that come about because of what occurs on this day. So let it be known that Mother Gaia sees it all and resonates to a different level of consciousness today.

Expect Benevolent Outcomes

53

Power of Intent

React. That is what you do. You react to surprise phone calls, to the mail, to the uncooperative agent at the other end of your phone line. Stop the negative reactions. You know how to design your days with your intention. Intention, once it is cognized, rules all. As you learn to speak it, feel the joy of it and re-visit it frequently, you will be amazed at your power. This has always been true but it is even faster and more obvious in this new energy. Know you can arrange your day, plan on synchronicity but ONLY as long as you know and can articulate your intent. And yes, as you get better at doing this you can continue to refine your expressions of intent saying them better and better until your days are merely chains of expressing and realizing everything that you want. So, as I have cautioned in the past, choose carefully where you place the energy of intent. You will soon see the outcomes and they can have 'unintended' consequences. So, as we start, we shall finish with an example: "Today I know and expect that all Universal elements will converge to deliver me the most benevolent outcomes and sustain my health, relationships and energy and abundance, so that I feel continued joy and love of all."

Bless the Water

54

Bless the Water

Water. As you know you are made of earth particles and water. While the formula H2O tells only part of the story, the other half is far more interesting. The bonds that hold water together are very loose. It takes but little, such as heat, to move them apart into less and less tightly bound forms. Literally, water has fluidity. But water has fluidity in all its states. In solid, liquid and gaseous form. And in the presence of earth molecules such as sodium and chloride. As you do not know through measurement, the energy flows around water can change it's aggregation of molecules. As you do know through sight, the application of different forms of emotive energies can change the crystalline structure of water as it forms into ice. Much like the latter example, your bodies, because they are so fluid and filled with water, respond very quickly to various energies including that which you yourself generate. For this reason it is important to keep the bodily fluids under the influence of positive emotion and not allow the films of hatred, over-excitement, distress influence the mind. For just as water that is blessed has healthful effects on the body, water that has been exposed, even when it is inside you, to negative emotions, does more damage than good.

So, if you wish to prepare and set your body to receive the benefits of water there are several things that can be done. First, bless the water as you hold it in your glass (made of glass is best) and impart it with love as you imbibe. For this practice alone will do much to assist your bodies in the renewal and healing that is necessary to maintain perfect health.

Another method is to view the water in a container and focus thoughts of joy, love, laughter, and other sentiments upon it. It will deliver those to you as you drink it. And lastly, though it will be rare that you arrange the optimal fields, expose your drinking water to magnetic fields. More than one is best, but even a single string of magnets will align the water to become more beneficial when you consume it. It has a field effect that allows the molecules to more easily penetrate cells, to wash free toxins and deliver them outside your bodies. It is also able to more efficiently transport nutrients to cells to make them more available for improved nourishment.

Do these things to be kind to your bodies, for it is typically in the Highest Good that you live a long, happy, healthy and pain-free life. All of you will benefit to some extent from these practices. And so it is.

55

Attention to Thoughts

Your comfort is of the essence. No man or woman can be in a state of joyous connection with Source when they are focused on pain, wants, things that bring no solace. All of My Children should pay attention only to the experiences they wish to repeat. So, if you have pain upon walking stairs walk on flat ground until you know not the pain anymore. Then attend only to how good it feels to walk. It is truth that conscious mind can and does have power over physical. However, you have established patterns that often hold their own strength because of repetition of wrong/unsuitable thinking. You know what your thoughts should be doing to ensure your well-being. Pay attention to everyone. Choose only those thoughts that feel good. Focus on what you want and teach that by demonstrating as such. Try...., no, DO this in the name of Christ for Christ the Life Source shows you how.

56

Breath Heals

There is life in breath. As your ancient practices of deep breathing, yoga, healing therapies and mental calming have known the breath is one of the keys of life. The breath contains more than just air or the gases you require for your bodies to live but it truly contains substance called "prana" by many, "chi" by others. This reflects the ancient knowing that there is an energizing, a flow of essence through the body when breathing is consciously and excessively called upon. This energy, or prana, can be called to flow into certain body parts with visualization and intent. It is necessary but not sufficient to cause healing. So, if there is intent to heal a broken bone, a bad stomach or sinus pain, the breath can be directed by seeing it flow and watching the healing. As long as there is proper nutrition, exercise and movement of the body and the proper fluid balance, there is no other reason than emotional scars that the body should not heal. And there are other ways to address and alleviate the effects of emotional scars. In this new energy, that is much more conducive to healing, use these tools to provide comfort and live a pain free existence. For it is only those who live comfortably in their bodies that have the freedom to engage their minds in higher level thoughts and pursuits. For the Highest Good to be realized by All, there needs to be peace in each one's countenance, not disrupted by the mental focus on pain.

Use this tool, daily if you must, until you no longer feel discomfort. You will be surprised and delighted for this tool will provide rapid and reliable healing. Healing from within that is as permanent as is the body.

Go in joy with this new knowledge.

Infuse your Thoughts With Love

57

Clear Intent

There is right. There is no such thing as wrong. For each of you comes to this Earth to make your own life and self and portrait. You do create your experiences as clearly as you create your song, your speech and your dance. It is with free choice and thoughts and words that you move the energies about you to congeal into physical matter. It is with thoughts, and faith that it will be so that you allow the people and forces to move circumstances to meet your needs. It is with intention that you steer your ship. Pure positive intention cannot be derailed. When it is mixed, unclear, for negative effects, it then becomes muddled. So, in your days ahead, most clearly formulate your intention in a clear, positive and direct way. Stick with it - don't change it every day. But know that if you continue in the faith of it, you will have it. If it brings joy, happiness and good to all, you will have it faster. As it comes, ensure you do not desecrate it with less than good intentions for how it is used. Be joyful and actively think and embrace the good of it. Shortly you will experience even greater alignment of people and things to bring more joy and Higher Good. Know, always, it is how you think and feel that creates or co-creates with the Universe. I, the Life Source create with the power of Love. You, too, can infuse your daily thoughts with love which is the most powerful way to move the energies of the Universe to align with your intentions. Then sit back and allow it to happen. Be joyful. Be kind. Be loving. And all will be handed to you on a "silver platter" for you are loved beyond measure, and can even direct or re-direct some of that force in your life. And it is so.

58

Seek for Yourself First

It is easy to love when you feel good. For that reason it becomes important for you to feel as good as you can every moment of each day. Many of you believe that it is selfish and wanton to seek your own comfort, and pleasure, and abundance, before that of another. I tell you now, that is not the case. You must seek for yourself first. You must feel good in your body - seek perfect health. You must feel that your needs are well taken care of - seek your prosperity. You must be comfortable sharing with others - seek your abundance. And, most importantly you must remain in a state of peace, calm and gentle knowing that all is well before you can look at that which surrounds you and emit a vibration of appreciation. You will be better able to really feel and send love to those around you when you know and feel the love that is being sent to you.

Keeping that flowing well of love moving is the source of life. And it is the way of manifesting the beautiful things of life. So, as you complete your daily readings, sit in quiet conversation with your God, sit in a meditative posture and breathe in the love energy. Just as the breath must move in, through you, and out of you, so must love to be an effective force in your world. So sit, My

Children, breathe in the love and as you exhale send those flows of loving essence to those you know and to those you don't know but who are in need. Your intention can easily direct your flows of loving energy to people and places in far away lands. You are all entangled with Mother Gaia and she with all of you. She, too, breathes and emits her love for you, through you. Go now and calm your thoughts and know that the love of the Universe flows with you.

59

Restructuring the World

Be bold. Dear Ones, be bold in your thoughts, in your dreams, in your expectations. For if not you, who will create the shape of this new world? As the spirit of Shiva lets much destruction reign, there must be those who have the vision of rebuilding. Even now, each of you are brought to the table to think of and re-align with your intentions. As you move forward in this new energy you have a window of opportunity to think big and bold and restructure everything from your politics, your social welfare systems and your care of each other across all ages. Think whether you will stand by and watch or lend your support, your wisdom to the youth who will lead this revolution of love, wisdom and productivity. They are a new breed and have little tolerance or patience for the way the world has evolved in the old energies. Be bold, my Dears, for you are on the brink - no, in the midst of a heavenly restructuring of your world. Think Big, so you can accomplish all that is needed. Think boldly so it can be done well and fast. Think in loving ways, feel compassion so that it will complete in the Highest Good for All. So be it. Be bold.

Bold and Free

END Volume 2

Please look for the publication of Volume 3

Printed in the United States
By Bookmasters